ESCAPE FROM THE TOWERS

Andra Serlin Abramson

with thanks to
Greg Trevor and Florence Engoran for their stories

 Crabtree Publishing Company

www.crabtreebooks.com

Crabtree Publishing Company

www.crabtreebooks.com   1-800-387-7650

Copyright © **2009 CRABTREE PUBLISHING COMPANY**.
All rights reserved. No part of this publication may be reproduced, stored in a retrieval system or be transmitted in any form or by any means, electronic, mechanical, photocopying, recording, or otherwise, without the prior written permission of Crabtree Publishing Company.

Author: Andra Serlin Abramson
Project editor: Ruth Owen
Project designer: Sara Greasley
Photo research: Lizzie Knowles
Proofreaders: Crystal Sikkens
Production coordinator:
    Katherine Kantor
Prepress technicians:
    Katherine Kantor, Ken Wright

With thanks to series editors Honor Head and Jean Coppendale, and consultant Mark J. Sachner.

Thank you to Lorraine Petersen and the members of nasen

**Published
in Canada
Crabtree Publishing**
616 Welland Ave.
St. Catharines, ON
L2M 5V6

**Published in the
United States
Crabtree Publishing**
PMB16A
350 Fifth Ave., Suite 3308
New York, NY 10118

Content development by Shakespeare Squared
www.ShakespeareSquared.com
First published in Great Britain in 2008 by ticktock Media Ltd,
2 Orchard Business Centre, North Farm Road,
Tunbridge Wells, Kent, TN2 3XF
Copyright © ticktock Entertainment Ltd 2008

Picture credits:
Alamy: Peter Horree: p. 5
Corbis: Sean Adair/Reuters: p. 16–17; Chris Collins: p. 10, 18;
    Erik Freeland: p. 26; Ann Giordano: p. 13; Rob Howard:
    cover; Lower Manhattan Development Corp: p. 31;
    Reuters: p. 25, 28, 29; Peter Turnley: p. 1
Getty Images: p. 2, 20–21, 24; AFP: p. 19
Jupiter Images: p. 23
PA Photos: John Labriola/AP: p. 22
Rex Features: Andrea Boohers: p. 27 (bottom); Heathcliff
    O'Malley: p. 27 (top); Sipa Press: p. 12
Shutterstock: p. 6
SuperStock: age fotostock: p. 8–9, Roderick Chen: p. 7;
    Emmanuel Faure: p. 4; Mike Ford: p. 14; Image Source:
    p. 11 (top); Lisette Le Bon: p. 15; PhotoAlto: p. 11 (bottom)

Every effort has been made to trace copyright holders, and we apologize in advance for any omissions. We would be pleased to insert the appropriate acknowledgments in any subsequent edition of this publication.

Library and Archives Canada Cataloguing in Publication

Abramson, Andra Serlin
    Escape from the towers / Andra Serlin Abramson.

(Crabtree contact)
Includes index.
ISBN 978-0-7787-3814-5 (bound).--ISBN 978-0-7787-3836-7 (pbk.)

    1. September 11 Terrorist Attacks, 2001--Juvenile literature.
2. World Trade Center (New York, N.Y.)--Juvenile literature.
3. Terrorism--United States--Juvenile literature. I. Title. II. Series.

HV6432.7.A27 2008   j974.7'1044   C2008-905954-9

Library of Congress Cataloging-in-Publication Data

Abramson, Andra Serlin.
    Escape from the towers / Andra Serlin Abramson.
        p. cm. -- (Crabtree contact)
    Includes index.
    ISBN-13: 978-0-7787-3836-7 (pbk. : alk. paper)
    ISBN-10: 0-7787-3836-1 (pbk. : alk. paper)
    ISBN-13: 978-0-7787-3814-5 (reinforced library binding : alk. paper)
    ISBN-10: 0-7787-3814-0 (reinforced library binding : alk. paper)
    1. September 11 Terrorist Attacks, 2001--Juvenile literature. 2.
Terrorism--United States--Juvenile literature. I. Title. II. Series.
    HV6432.7.A264 2009
    974.7'1044--dc22
                                2008039404

Contents

CHAPTER 1
JUST ANOTHER DAY

Tuesday, September 11, 2001,
was a bright, sunny day.
The skies were blue.

In New York City, the streets were filled with people.

Children were going to school.
People were heading to work.

The towers of the **World Trade Center** sparkled in the sunlight.

The World Trade Center was a group of seven office buildings. The two tallest buildings were called the Twin Towers. The towers stood side-by-side. Each building was 110 **stories** high.

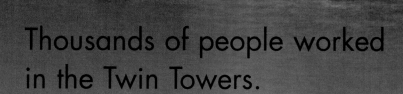

Twin Towers

Thousands of people worked in the Twin Towers.

HIJACKED

Nearly 200 miles (320 kilometers) from New York City, it was a busy morning at Logan International Airport in Boston.

On the runway, two planes were ready for take-off.

American Airlines Flight 11 and United Airlines Flight 175 were heading for Los Angeles, California.

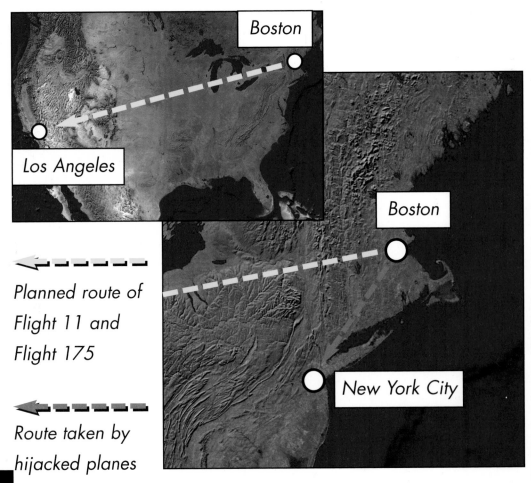

Planned route of Flight 11 and Flight 175

Route taken by hijacked planes

Soon after take-off, Flight 11 was **hijacked** by **terrorists**. The hijackers took control of the **cockpit**. They flew the plane toward New York City.

Reconstruction *of hijackers in the plane's cockpit*

Minutes later, Flight 175 was hijacked by terrorists. The terrorists also flew the plane toward New York City.

In New York City, Greg Trevor was hard at work at the World Trade Center.

Greg was working on the 68th floor of the North Tower.

Florence Engoran was heading to work. She rode the elevator up to the 55th floor of the South Tower.

It was a normal day. But in five minutes, nothing would be the same again.

North Tower

South Tower

CHAPTER 3

THE FIRST IMPACT

At 8:46 a.m., Greg Trevor finished a phone call. He stood up to stretch his legs.

At that moment, there was a huge crash. American Airlines Flight 11 slammed into Greg's building.

North Tower

The plane hit the North Tower about 20 floors above Greg's office.

Greg remembers hearing a loud noise. Then he heard an explosion.

Greg felt the building sway back and forth. He saw glass and paper falling outside his window. He heard alarm bells ringing.

Reconstruction

08:50 The air began to fill with smoke.

Greg and the other workers knew they had to leave the building immediately.

The elevators were not working because of the crash. The group of workers started the long walk down hundreds of stairs.

Reconstruction

08:55

Outside on the streets and in nearby buildings, people watched in horror.

The North Tower was in flames.
Parts of the building were falling to the ground.
Thick, black smoke was filling the sky.

Across New York City, fire alarms and police radios were calling police, firefighters, and ambulance crews to the **scene**.

Within minutes of the crash, hundreds of rescue workers were heading to the World Trade Center.

CHAPTER 4

THE SECOND IMPACT

08:46

Florence Engoran reached her office on the 55th floor of the South Tower.

Florence did not see nor hear the plane hit the North Tower, but people in her office were talking about it.

Florence and the other people in the office decided they should begin work. But soon, huge bits of concrete and burning papers were falling past Florence's office window.

Reconstruction

"I didn't go back to pick up my bag. I turned right around and ran to the fire steps."
Florence Engoran

On the South Tower stairs, people were scared.

A woman behind Florence screamed,
"Go faster! Go faster!"

Florence shouted back,
"I'm going as fast as I can!"

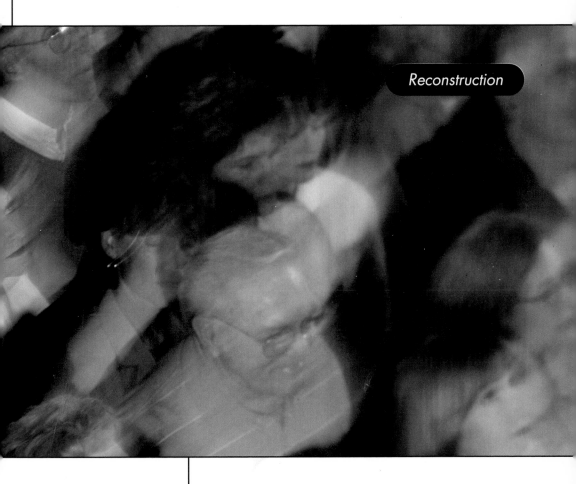

Reconstruction

By now, the disaster in
New York City was being
shown live on TV news
shows around the world.

09:03

As millions of people around the world watched, United Airlines Flight 175 crashed into the South Tower.

Flight 175

By now, Florence Engoran had reached the 20th floor.

"I held onto the handrail. The **impact** knocked people over if you didn't hold on. The building moved two to three meters. Everyone stopped dead because the building was swaying so badly."

The plane crashed into floors 87 to 93.

South Tower

CHAPTER 5

INSIDE THE SOUTH TOWER

09:05 Inside the South Tower, people began to panic.

"The lights went out. Concrete and dust started to fill the stairwell. We were breathing it in. People started to scream. No one was moving. I could smell the jet fuel. It smelled like petrol."
Florence Engoran

09:50

At last, Florence made it down to the first floor. The police were waiting at the bottom of the stairs.

"Run!" The police yelled.

Florence ran as fast as she could.

When she turned around, she was shocked by what she saw. Both towers were in flames. Pieces of them were falling to the ground. Florence kept running. She knew she had to get away from the buildings.

09:59

The jet fuel from the planes caused huge fireballs inside the towers. The fire was so hot it made the steel columns inside the towers melt.

At 9:59 a.m., the South Tower **collapsed**. Millions of tons of steel and concrete crashed down. People in the streets ran to escape being crushed by the collapsing tower.

CHAPTER 6

INSIDE THE NORTH TOWER

Greg Trevor had been carefully making his way down the stairs of the North Tower.

"I wasn't scared at first," Greg remembers. Nobody knew the South Tower had collapsed.

Every now and then, the people on the stairs moved over to make way for firefighters. The firefighters were heading up the stairs toward the fire.

Finally, Greg and the other people reached the fourth floor of the North Tower.

 **10:10**

They were shocked to find that the emergency door was jammed. Greg and the others were trapped.

The stairs were filled with smoke and concrete dust from the collapsed South Tower. The lights went out. It was hard to breathe. A stream of water ran down the stairs.

"It felt like we were wading through a dark, dirty, fast river—at night, in the middle of a forest fire."
Greg Trevor

10:15 For the first time, Greg was afraid he would not make it out alive.

Greg whispered a prayer, "Lord, please let me see my family again."

Minutes passed. On the other side of the door, the police were working to open it. Finally the door opened.

A police officer yelled, "Run for the exit!"

Outside the building, the air was filled with dust. Greg felt like he was walking through a dirty snowstorm.

At 10:28 a.m. a loud rumble drowned out all other sounds.

The North Tower collapsed.

CHAPTER 7

NEW YORK CITY'S SADDEST DAY

After the buildings collapsed, people stared at the **skyline**. There was an empty space where the Twin Towers used to be.

People were shocked and dazed. Strangers joined hands with strangers. They hugged each other. People cried.

On New York City's saddest day, New Yorkers came together. They helped each other as they never had before.

The towers that were once 110 stories high were now a twisted mound of metal. Everything inside was crushed into dust. Firefighters spent many days working to put out all the fires.

Rescue workers began searching through the rubble. Using machines, dogs, and even their bare hands, they searched for **survivors**.

The world changed forever on September 11, 2001.

At the time, no one knew how many people had been killed. All the world knew was that many families had lost loved ones.

At the scene, friends and relatives left photos of missing loved ones hoping someone had seen them.

At least 2,751 people were killed in New York City on September 11, 2001. All 147 people on the two planes died. The other **victims** were the people in the towers and rescue workers.

Police officers, ambulance crews, and firefighters rushed to the scene to help. On this tragic day, 412 of these brave people were killed—most when the towers fell. Without their bravery, many more people may have died.

Greg and Florence were two of the survivors. For them, and millions of people around the world, the tragic events of September 11th will forever be a day to remember the innocent lives that were lost.

cockpit The compartment where the pilot and crew flies the airplane

collapse To fall down or crumble into pieces

hijack To take over and control a plane or vehicle by force

impact When one thing hits another

Pentagon A five-sided building that is the headquarters of the United States Department of Defense. The Pentagon is in Arlington, Virginia, USA

reconstruction An image created to show what happened during an event. Reconstruction images are used in some places in this book. This is because no photographs are available of a particular event or moment in time

scene The place where an action or event takes place

skyline The shape of the buildings in a city when seen against the sky

story A level or floor in a building

survivor A person who is still alive after an event or accident in which they might have been killed

terrorist A person who tries to frighten people or governments into doing what he or she wants by using violence or threatening to use violence

victim A person who is hurt or killed

World Trade Center A group of seven office buildings in New York City. The World Trade Center included the Twin Towers.

Two other US planes were hijacked on September 11. One plane hit the **Pentagon**, near Washington, D.C. The other crashed in a field in Pennsylvania. The passengers on this plane tried to take back control from the hijackers. In total, 2,994 people died in the attacks, including 19 terrorists.

The place where the Twin Towers stood is now known as "Ground Zero." A park with a memorial will be built there. The memorial will be called "Reflecting Absence." The names of everyone who died at the World Trade Center will be listed there.

This is a model of the memorial "Reflecting Absence."

READ MORE ONLINE

www.911digitalarchive.org/
Stories and images from the events of September 11, 2001

www.pbs.org/wgbh/buildingbig/wonder/structure/world_trade.html
Information about the construction and collapse of the
World Trade Center Twin Towers

Publisher's note to educators and parents:
Our editors have carefully reviewed these websites to ensure that they are suitable for children. Many websites change frequently, however, and we cannot guarantee that a site's future contents will continue to meet our high standards of quality and educational value. Be advised that children should be closely supervised whenever they access the Internet.